Matrix of Bees, Stars, and Humans

Written by: Leandra Purvis
Photographs by: Ethan Swanberg

Copyright © 2018 by Leandra Purvis & Ethan Swanberg

First Edition

CONTENTS

Foreword

To eat,
To sleep,
To breath.
This is being alive.

To feel,
To love,
To create.
This is living,
This is life.

This is being human.

August 12, 2018

Hello

I stand here listening to the last goodbyes.
From those who are too young to know,
But too old to cry.
I stand here proudly with the wind in my eyes.
Who would have known we couldn't keep these close ties?

I want to keep my head held high,
As I leave to my grave with a sorrow-filled mind.
No one will know just how hard I tried,
For I kept it all in, protecting their pride.

Please say "hello" for me when I wouldn't.
Please say "I love you" to those whom I couldn't.

Hold them close,
Please
Please for me.
But let them breathe, they need to be free.

Now I must go,
But don't say goodbyes,
This can't be the end,
No no, it is never the end for me.

The Mute Prophet and The Alcoholic

I cried at dawn.
Through my tears I saw the end of life
Through my tears I saw the birth of a saint
Through my tears I saw the reflection of myself.

I walked down a dark alleyway at dusk.
At the end I saw an exit
At the end I thought I saw hope
At the end I found a decaying open sign and a one-way ticket.

I rode down an empty street in the dead of night.
I passed a gas station with a homeless man who sat in the gutter
reciting Whitman
I passed an abandoned church still burnt by sins of the holy
I passed by a prison where moans of the innocent and guilty were
one and the same.

The past cries like an alcoholic
The future walks as a mute prophet
The present rides alone
We have everything
And we are nothing.

Elbows and Hips

The trees they swayed as the guitars played.
I felt I was in a movie as the sweet hymns were laid.

But unlike a movie it was real and it was true.
Breaths mingled in the damp air as bodies glided against one another.
Elbows knocking as hips collided.
The Lead with his hand on the small of the Follows back,
Guiding her in a new direction each second,
Yet making it all fit together in one smooth wave.

The band became louder as the skies grew darker.
Drinks were passed around and lanterns were lit,
Allowing the dancers to cast shadows upon the floors.

People began singing the songs the band played out,
Till they were filled with drinks and love and laughter alike.

Bright in smiles,
Bright in laughter,
Bright in love.

The song ended and a lead took my attention from my stars.
Off I went the starry night,
Elbows knocking,
Hips colliding,
Breath mingling.

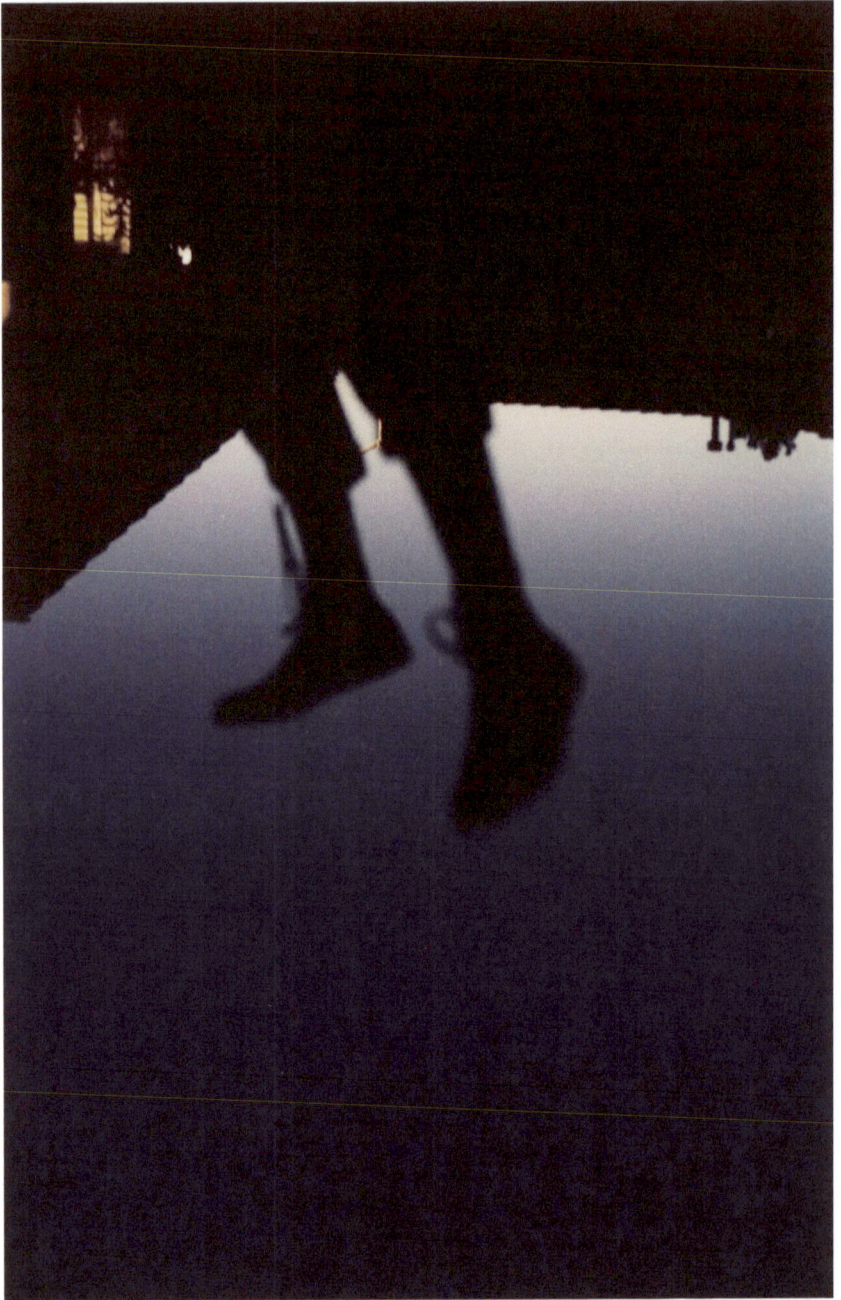

Moonlight

I dance beneath the crowded trees,
Where the birds sing loudly and the deer run free.
I wave my arms around,
Howling with glee into the vast plains of green.
This earth is so lovely.

I lay down in the grass,
Singing the song of the wind as the leaves tickle my skin.
The trees soon join me in my melody,
The branches swaying, dancing along to the rhythm in my hips.

I never shall choose to leave this wondrous land of mine.
Only here can one feel truly connected with earth and sky.
The unnecessary drama of life's busy race,
Seems to not even exist in this soft, peaceful place.

So I will sit here and listen to the birds and the bees,
Staying until the moon climbs high up over me.
Only then will I sleep, in the soft, lazy grass.
With a willow bending over me,
The leaves forming shadows from the moon's light,
Like sun through holy panes of colored glass.

What a gorgeous day it was I chose.
The day to roam and experience life away from home.
Where no one could touch me,
And my sight was not obscured,
By the fast city lights in my fast city life.

Midnight Blues

Wrought with desire,
They were torn from their homes.
Dragged out of their beds in the middle of the night

Then sent out in the streets.

Forced to
search
search
search.
For what?
They did not know.
But they needed to go.
This force clawed at them
Made their skin crawl
Still, they kept looking.

Up and down the hollow, dusty streets they spread like ink.
So many left to wander
So many souls not yet gone under.

Feeling alone as the wind blew them down the empty bridges
They continued on their journey
In hopes to find what lit their fire.

On and on they went around,
Nothing in sight, nothing to be found.
Dangerous was this feeling,

Knowing not what you want
But needing to have it.

Oh, but wait until those somber fires burst into the air once more.
They will return to their homes,
And as they recycle their clothes, their smiles, and their minds,
They'll forget what drives them wild.

At least until the darkness swallows their world once again,
And they are forced to
search
search
search.
Search for what they desire,
Like a mad man crawling through barbed wire.

I Have Loved You Always

I crave a touch I cannot have.
The purist of impure thoughts flood my visions,
For I wish to see what could possibly be.

What it would be like,
To hold you in my arms,
To run my hands through your hair,
To see you in the dawn's new light with your eyes closed and your
mouth parted so slightly.

When will you come to dig me out from the flowers I have buried
myself under?
The flowers where I lay in hopes to appear sturdy and strong to all
those who pass by.

Day by day, my stems become weaker,
fall has come to take my petals away,
Leaving me helpless to the rain that cries down upon me.
Soon, I will begin to wilt and be unable to free myself from this
grave in the ground.

But for now I must wait,
Hoping you will see me one day,
In my wilted beauty.
A love that will grow and feel weightless, yet come down with the
force of gravity.

In my heart I have loved you always.

Even now as I do not know the sound of your voice or of your
beating heart,
Even now as I do not know the curves of your face or the color of
your skin,
Even now as I do not know your name,
I have loved you always.

Lay With Me

Soon there was a field of tall grass,
The grey growing into green and yellow as the light shifted and
fire burst into the air.
Wading through, they slid their fingers across the ridged edges of
the tall blades
The breeze whispering sweet nothings into lost ears.

"Lay me down upon the green grass growing"
His fingers ran through her soft hair splayed upon his chest
She watched the clouds dance across the sky
Casting shadows on the land below.

Birds cooed into the dewy air
He let out a sigh which turned to a sob.
She pressed his hand to her heart
While turning her ear to his,
Listening for the thundering beat inside,
Waiting for the storm to pass.

Glazed

You ever hear a poem and it hits you right to the core?
It's like something you've never heard before,
It twists you up and turns you around,
Chews you up and spits you back out.

You gain your balance and open your eyes,
And, my god, the world never looked this way in past times!
There's colors you've never seen,
Sights beyond your wildest dreams!

You look to your left and you look to your right,
There are people all around who seem nowhere bound.
They mumble and fumble, feeling around,
Trying to find the best gimmicks in town.

But now you know the trick, and you know it good,
The true things in life, don't come from these hoods.
Not from shopping mall alleys or liquor store valleys,
Nor from media pages or celebrity crazes.
Not from bubblegum pop or secondhand shops,
And definitely not from the ones they call gods.

But now you don't know what your peers see and think,
So where will you fit, inside this old, messy rink?
You can't sell your soul for life's Pretty Pink,
To be a glazed-over face who looks empty and blinks.

You will not be one who sits there and states,
"Wow,
Look at these clothes,
These cars,
These gates,
I'll give you body and mind if you give me a taste."

Or one who takes pictures to post them and write,
"Look at my skin glow,
Look at my shine,
Look at my laugh,
Look at my grand ol' time."

Now you know, this isn't real,
And soon you'll find people who have the same deal.
They won't catch a trend just to cash in real quick,
Like those with no morals who think that they're slick.
A work-mutt like you, who sees life's bigger goals,
And in the end of it all comes out with their souls.

From this poem, you see, it's like you learned how to live.
You learned that life is dirty, it's dark, and it's grim.
But there's beauty in it too, though it sometimes seems dim.
You've just got to keep on like a bird in the wind,
Life will keep kicking, but now you know you can win.

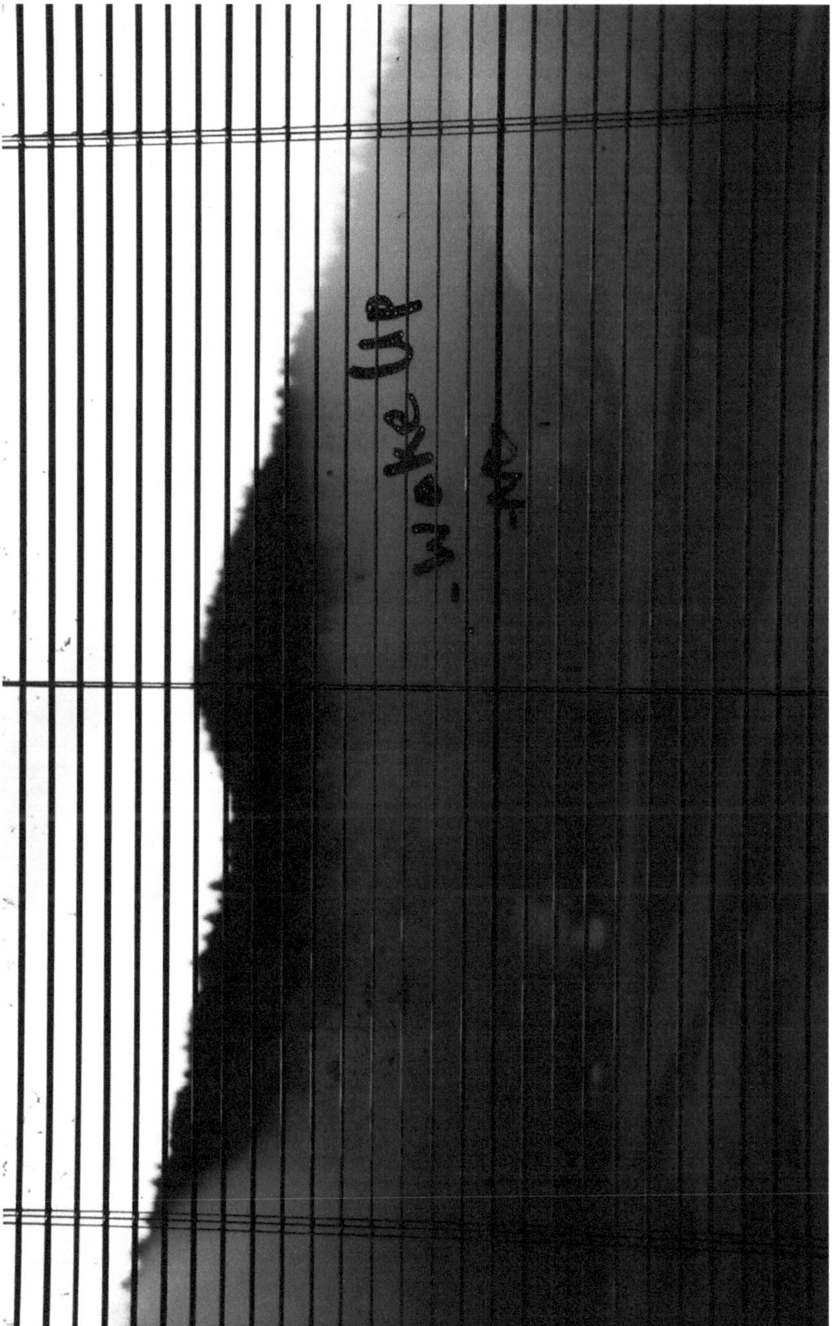
wake UP

Deadly

What is it about human touch?
Something so peculiar it slips off the tongue,
Trying to make two into one.
With the possibility of being so deadly,
It's terrifying and exhilarating, all in one medley.

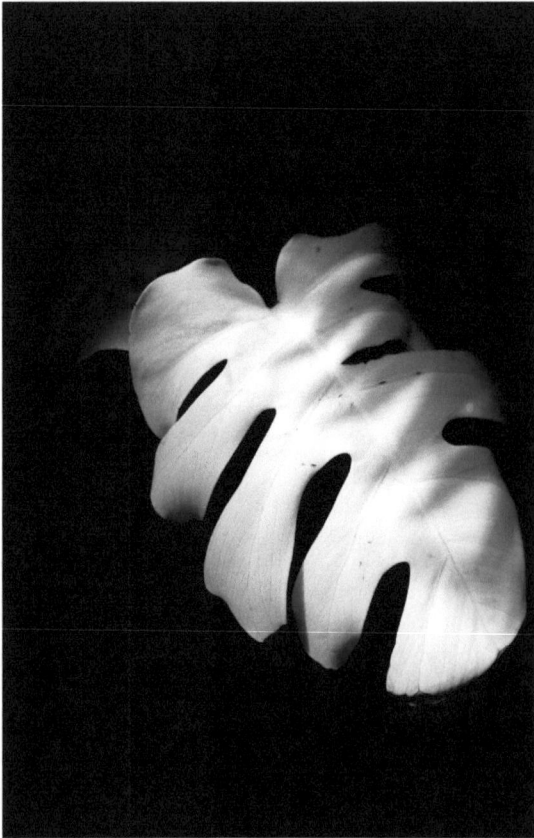

Factory Life

What is happening in our world?
We have turned into a factory,
In our hurry to produce the next best weapon,
We pump mushroom clouds of fear into the air.

This fear seeps into our blood.
It runs through us from head to toe,
Flowing out of our fingertips in a constant stream,
Like water going over the mountain's edge.

Our children breathe this in from a young age.
Instead of learning to live, they are learning to hide.
To be afraid of what could be around the corner.

This is no way to live,
But it is surely a faster way to die.

Folktales of Love and Sorrow

"Sing us a song."
They said to me.
"One of great love, and of great misery."

"I cannot sing of love or sorrow to you,"
I spoke oh so quietly,
"As I cannot sing to you your story for free."

Confused, they looked to and between.
I took no charge in order to sing,
So why should I ask they pay me a fee?

"Why it's not money I ask.
No no sir, it would not be.
The price I ask is one of life and liberty."

"For I could sing, but you could not grasp.
You, yourself must feel the pain of love and loss in order to really
see.
This is something that does not come for free.

"Once you have lived, I will play for thee.
My rhymes will burst forth and set your mind free.
They will show you tales of lust and love that burned hot as the
sun,
And stories of grief that will make you want to dig your own
grave,
instead of feeling the pain dealt to their days.

"But in these stories I bring to you,
I give you only the outline of what could be.
You give it the color that only you can see.
You fill it with names and faces of those you knew,
Showing that the greatest tales of love and misery,
Are the ones that come from you."

My Love

If you choose me
Fall in love as you would fall into your casket
But dig your grave for yourself
And I will dig mine by it
Wave goodbye to the sky we know
As friends and family put us under
From our hearts a swarm of bees
And from our minds; sweet, sweet honey

My Dearest Desert

I sit unwound beneath the lovely sky.
It calls to me as I look out upon the dusty desert.
There are hues of rosa and naranja and verde azulado.
It fades into azul oscuro where the moon begins to rise above the mountains.

The tumbleweeds sway in the gentle breeze.
Looking soft to the touch,
but truly harsh as a wasp.

The sand is cool,
Colder than you'd expect.
Lizards run over and under rocks to find a place to rest.

I've lived my life here, from birth to old age.
Met my first love,
Played my first games.
Became caught up in the world of trivial flames.

But none of it matters now, as I look out among the planes.
My spirit still young but my body has aged.
It holds me here in this material world.
Where we fight over everything and nothing at all.

Only here I find peace,
Only now in this time.
The spirit of the desert flowing around me.
The wind whispering sweet nothings in my ears.

It's drawing my soul out of my corpse.
Hollowing me out until the wind begins to play me like a flute.
I don't mind much though, I make beautiful music.

Te dejo.

Poison

I have things to say and they're stuck in my head,
I feel I'm being strangled as I lay here in bed.

I cannot free them, no matter how hard I try.
They run to the edge of my tongue looking over the cliff,
Daring themselves to jump off the bridge.

But they won't take the leap,
No, they won't even try.
But it's all an illusion like pigs flying by.

The end is not near.
My death will not come,
If I swallow my pride and spit out my thumb.

Meet Me in the Early Morning

Meet me in the early morning
When the stars still dance and die
When the sun hasn't yet come out to try
When the same old face still says "do not cry"

Meet me in the early morning
Before the children of love and hate rise
Before the air is filled with cruelty and lies
Before the lovers say their last hellos and first goodbyes

Meet me in the early morning
So I can say what I truly mean
So my mind is still full fantasy's dreams
So I still have faith in love that is clean

Mother Nature

We came from her,
Soon we will go back to her.

"Save her" we plead
Yet we sit and watch her bleed.

Still she sits and softly sings in the wind,
The daisies lazily swaying under her hymn.

Together we ignore her,
But oh-
How we adore her.

Slowly she rots,
Yet-
We stop not.

So she calls to us, crying out,
"How do you breath me in and out,
How do you feel me under your feet,
And not protect me?"

When will we realize?
We came from her,
Soon we will go back to her.

Movie Night

Evil hides behind heavens gates.
Close your eyes and sit and wait.
The hypocrisy of our lives will soon be agape.

We'll sit and watch it on a screen in the dark.
Good and evil will fight like larks.
We'll root for one, hoping the other will fade out into the crystal ark.
Into he who hangs above us piercing through the heart of the dark.

But we are like children watching a movie,
White versus black, good versus evil, a hero versus a villain.
The battle to end all battles.
That is what we thought we saw.
That is what they told us we saw.

In reality, it is brother fighting brother.
A twin versus a twin.
Man versus himself in a bloody battle to win.

When will we realize this movie isn't fiction at all?
It's simply the replay of our lives like the rolling of a ball.
Man fights man, leading us to our downfall.
Leaving only destruction and ruin for the mothers and children who call.

Maybe soon we'll learn from them.
To try to love, not tear the hem.
But, one mistake and we'll end up in their same place once again.

To My Loved Ones

Oh mama, I plead.
Don't cry for me as you see on T.V.,
I'll be back soon, just wait and see.

Oh papa, I sigh.
Do not let the voices in the night swallow your life.
Let your knife shine and make them think twice.

Oh sister, I cry.
Choose wisely your path to tread.
For you never want it to be the one you dread.

Oh brothers, I whisper.
Look out upon the sunset, see what nature has to give you.
Do not take anything for granted, as it could come back to bite
you.

As for myself, I must go.
I'll see you in the moonlight,
Like a mirage in close sight.

But don't feel lonely, my loved ones.
My spirit will dance above you,
I will never choose to leave you.

The Singer of Songs

He sang to me from
the stars like wind
blowing through the
chimes hanging on my
patio at dusk.

When his voice comes
to you it feels as
though it goes straight
through,
Like a bullet piercing
your skin,
It's a pain that comes
from within.

That is what they do, good singers.
They do not make you feel as though they are singing to you.
They make you feel as though the voice comes from inside you.

Their songs, they dissect you.

Give you memories of something you never went through.
Show you who you are and how you grew.

Then they rearrange you.

They put you back together piece by piece as if you never came
undone.

But something isn't right.

You aren't the same as before.
You speak differently,
You walk differently,
You see the world differently.

Your inner core has been changed.
There's a new piece to the puzzle of,
"who am I?"

But as you add on this new piece, three more spots become
available to fill.
You think they give you the answers but really they only give you
more questions to mill.

But questions are just as good as answers.
So he continues to sing,
And we continue to listen.

Giving us bits and pieces of life itself,
Tearing our eyes away from the T.V. on the shelf.

He fills our minds with wonderful scenes,
Shows us how beautiful our souls do truly seem.
So sing on and show us all what we can be.

The Portrait of Mankind

I see the echo of time.
It ripples through me like the waves of the ocean.
Past, present, future.
They all slip in and out, and up and down until one cannot tell
which is which.

I lie back and let the sensation wash over me.
As I watch time go by I feel the emotions that go with it.
Love, hate, fear.
They, as well, know no bounds and come and go as they please,
Leaving me helpless to their tugs at my sleeve.

"It's beautiful isn't it?" I whisper to myself.
The vast expanse of humanity going by instantaneously.

A mother holds her new born baby.
Boys are sent off to fight for a cause they don't understand.
A young girl dances with her crush.
White men lynch a black teen.
A blind girl sees a rainbow.
Monks set themselves on fire.
Kids run through the streets while colored powder hangs in the air.
Men are tried for crimes against humanity.
Two lovers dance in the rain.
A cult commits a mass suicide, 918 men, women, and children
took their last breath.

There's a balance to everything.
Every great beauty comes with great sacrifice.
But these two do not blend together forming muddy colors.
They create depth and dimension,
Using light and dark to paint the most magnificent portrait.

This portrait tells the story of humanity.
A heart wrenching, yet beautiful story.

Matrix of Bees

I am of the trees that surround me.
I am of the dirt beneath my feet.
I am of the sky, the moon, and the stars above me.
And I am of the people on this earth with me.

I realize this so clearly now,
As I stand in this field watching the world go by around me.

The bees float softly and swiftly through the air.
From flower to flower they gently glide.
The flowers themselves swaying so lightly in the wind.
The wind, he blows the flowers and the trees and the grass that lies around my feet.

Barefoot, now I sit, my feet freely able to feel the energy the earth has to offer.
The grass feels soft beneath my toes, and every now and then a small insect makes it's way over them.

I can see people dancing in the distance.
They dance to the beat of a drum.
Soft then heavy, the rhythm persistent.
Girls in dresses twirl, while boys clap and run to the pounding percussion.
Their love and joy so pure, they seem to glow with it.
I can almost feel it from where I sit.

Matrix of Bees, Stars, and Humans

The sun soon begins to set,
Beautiful shades of orange and indigo and rose flood my senses.
The smell of lavender fills my nose, calming me even more.

Soon the dancers upon the hill light a fire,
The smoke rises in the air, dancing, as the boys and girls had
before.

My feet travel deeper into the earth,
Feeling the dirt between my toes.

It seems the bees have gone to sleep now,
'Rest peacefully my small ones', I whisper.
The wind itself has even seemed to calm,
Weary from the days activities.
The flowers' petals now sitting languidly upon their stems.

The stars now shine down upon us,
Sparkling in all their wondrous glory.
It's comforting knowing one day I will be among them.

For now though, I'll fall asleep.
Knowing that even here, in this life, I am of the bees, the stars, and
the humans that surround me.

The White Dove

My troubles run into the fog of the night.
I see their shadows dance past the trees on the right,
Where the center of town divides into darkness and light.
My eyes flutter shut
as the image of Christ's crucifixion seeps into my blood.
I cannot be who they want me to be,
Will I take the leap I hope will set them free?

No,
I can't, I won't.
They don't want me for me,
They want me to be who they think they see.
I am a ghost, a shadow, a shell.
Hollow to the bone, their voices course through me like the
lightning in hell.

"Where do you lie?" They whisper in my ear.
"To the left? Or to the right?"
"You don't own me." I spit back, feeling fire rise inside.
"But you must choose," they hiss, voices cold as ice,
"be on the right side of history."

The "right side" is the winning side.
Has been and will be forever.
The story has changed but the people will never.

Those who lost will go to their grave,
Hearing the bells of the evil and brave.
Their voices crushed by the foot of the loud,

Who never open their minds but seem so proud.

Speaking to the crowd they preach of the evils below,
Little do they know, they soon too, will be lying in the cold, dark,
unknown.

My eyes flutter open and the shadows still dance.
I'm standing in the dark with the light flying past.
I try to hide though I know it's no use,
They will all find me and soon I must choose.

But I will stand for what's good, what's moral and true,
I cannot say everything, but something will do.
I will speak my mind, through and through,
No voices above commanding my tune.

Humanity will weep and the white dove will cry,
But in the end, serenity will be found and love will reign like the
demanding sun in the sky.

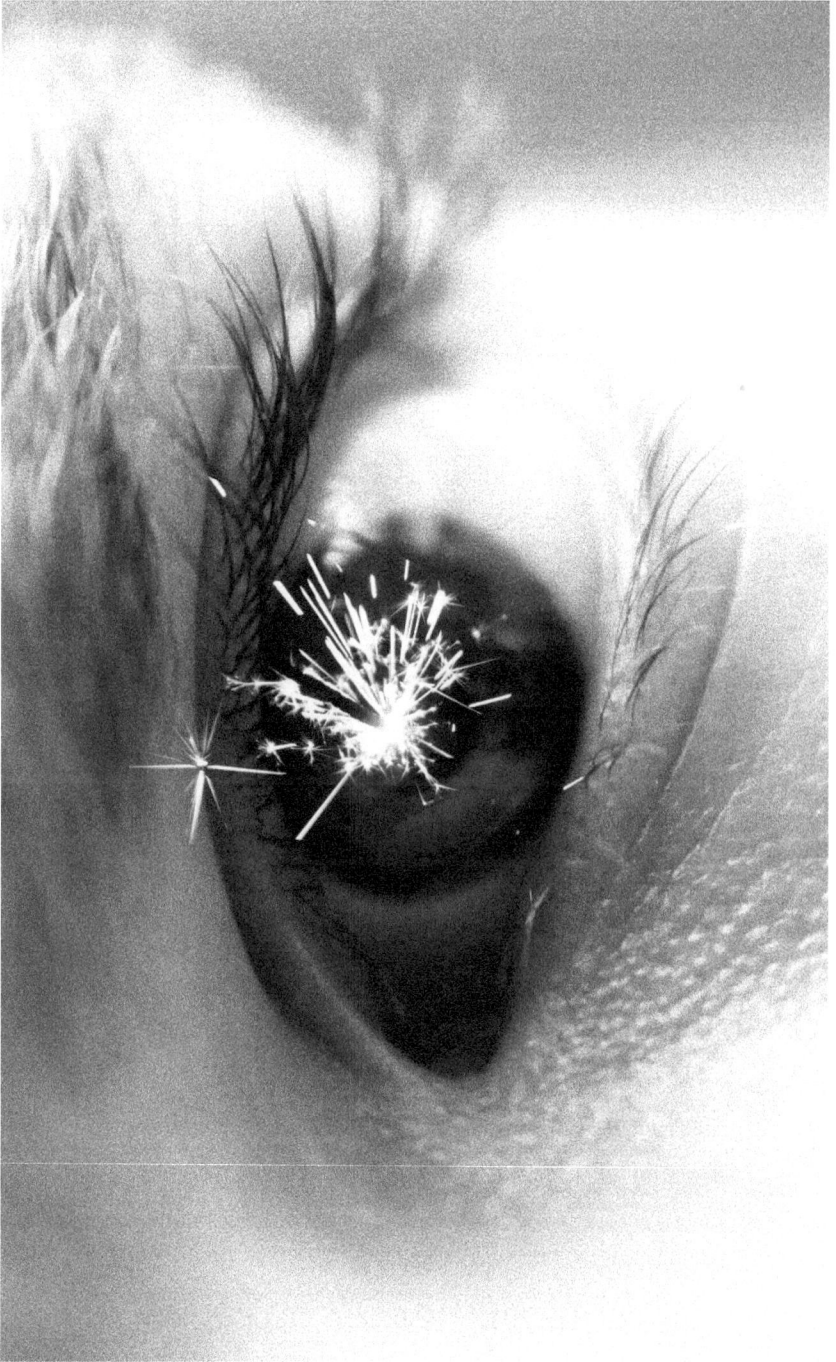